▣ DORLING KINDERSLEY *READERS*

Level 1
Beginning to Read

A Day at Greenhill Farm
Truck Trouble
Tale of a Tadpole
Surprise Puppy!
Duckling Days
A Day at Seagull Beach
Whatever the Weather
Busy Buzzy Bee
Big Machines
Wild Baby Animals
LEGO: Trouble at the Bridge
A Bed for Winter
Born to be a Butterfly

Level 2
Beginning to Read Alone

Dinosaur Dinners
Fire Fighter!
Bugs! Bugs! Bugs!
Slinky, Scaly Snakes!
Animal Hospital
The Little Ballerina
Munching, Crunching, Sniffing
    and Snooping
The Secret Life of Trees
Winking, Blinking, Wiggling
    and Waggling
Astronaut – Living in Space
LEGO: Castle Under Attack!
Twisters!
Holiday! Celebration Days around
    the World

Level 3
Reading Alone

Spacebusters
Beastly Tales
Shark Attack!
Titanic
Invaders from Outer Space
Movie Magic
Plants Bite Back!
Time Traveler
Bermuda Triangle
Tiger Tales
Aladdin
Heidi
LEGO: Mission to the Arctic
Zeppelin – The Age of
    the Airship
Spies

Level 4
Proficient Readers

Days of the Knights
Volcanoes
Secrets of the Mummies
Pirates!
Horse Heroes
Trojan Horse
Micromonsters
Going for Gold!
Extreme Machines
Flying Ace – The Story of
    Amelia Earhart
Robin Hood
Black Beauty
LEGO: Race for Survival
Free at Last! The Story of
    Martin Luther King, Jr.
Joan of Arc
Spooky Spinechillers

A Note to Parents

Dorling Kindersley Readers is a compelling new program for beginning readers, designed in conjunction with leading literacy experts, including Dr. Linda Gambrell, President of the National Reading Conference and past board member of the International Reading Association.

Beautiful illustrations and superb full-color photographs combine with engaging, easy-to-read stories to offer a fresh approach to each subject in the series. Each *Dorling Kindersley Reader* is guaranteed to capture a child's interest while developing his or her reading skills, general knowledge, and love of reading.

The four levels of *Dorling Kindersley Readers* are aimed at different reading abilities, enabling you to choose the books that are exactly right for your child:

Level 1 – Beginning to read
Level 2 – Beginning to read alone
Level 3 – Reading alone
Level 4 – Proficient readers

The "normal" age at which a child begins to read can be anywhere from three to eight years old, so these levels are intended only as a general guideline.

No matter which level you select, you can be sure that you are helping your child learn to read, then read to learn!

Dorling DK Kindersley

LONDON, NEW YORK, SYDNEY, DELHI, PARIS,
MUNICH, and JOHANNESBURG

A DORLING KINDERSLEY BOOK
www.dk.com

Produced by Southern Lights
Custom Publishing

For Dorling Kindersley
Publisher Andrew Berkhut
Executive Editor Andrea Curley
Art Director Tina Vaughan
Photographer Howard L. Puckett

Reading Consultant
Linda Gambrell, Ph.D.

First American Edition, 2001
00 01 02 03 04 05 10 9 8 7 6 5 4 3 2 1
Published in the United States by Dorling Kindersley Publishing, Inc.
95 Madison Avenue, New York, New York 10016

Published in Great Britain by Dorling Kindersley Limited.

Library of Congress Cataloging-in-Publication Data

Hayward, Linda.
   A day in the life of a firefighter / by Linda Hayward.
   1st American ed.
   Audience:"Level 1, pre-school-grade 1."
   p. cm. -- (Dorling Kindersley readers)
   ISBN 0-7894-7366-6   ISBN 0-7894-7365-8 (pbk.)
   1. Fire extinction--Juvenile literature. [1. Fire fighters. 2. Fire
extinction. 3. Occupations.] I. Title. II. Series.

TH9148 .H39 2001
628.9'25--dc21   00-055538

Printed and bound in China by L. Rex Printing Co., Ltd.

The characters and events in this story are fictional and do not repre-
sent real persons or events. The author would like to thank Fire Chief
Frank Kovarik for his help. Special thanks to Fire Chief Robert Ezekiel,
City of Mountain Brook Fire Department, Mountain Brook, Alabama.

see our complete
catalog at
www.dk.com

DK DORLING KINDERSLEY *READERS*

BEGINNING
1
TO READ

A Day in the Life of a Firefighter

Written by Linda Hayward

DK

A Dorling Kindersley Book

Rob Green packs clean
clothes and says good-bye
to his family.
Rob is a firefighter.

 8:00 a.m.

At the fire station
he puts his clothes
in a locker.
Rob is on duty
for 24 hours.

Chief Myers gives the firefighters jobs for the day.

In case of fire, Rob is on rescue. Rob gets other jobs, too. Check the hoses and the nozzles. Cook supper.

nozzle

"A new restaurant needs to be inspected this morning," Chief Myers says. "And a second-grade class is coming to visit after lunch."

Rob checks. Nozzles
change the way the water
sprays out of the hose. All
of the nozzles are working.

Pete turns on
the engine.
Is there
enough gas?

Luis checks the oil level.

 10:30 a.m.

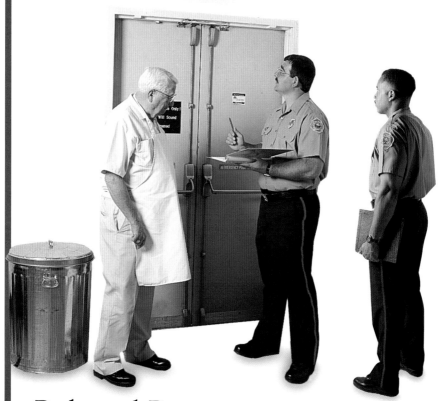

Rob and Pete inspect the restaurant. Is the fire exit light on?

fire exit

Where is the fire
extinguisher?

Do the sprinklers
work?

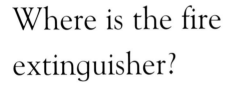

sprinkler

12:00 p.m.

It is lunch time.

Luis tells about
his fishing trip.
He caught enough to share.
Later, Rob will cook
the fish for supper.

1:30 p.m.

siren

Ms. Hill's class visits the fire station. Where is the siren?

Rob shows the class what he wears to a fire. This is the air pack.

air pack

"Remember!" Pete says. "In a room full of smoke, stay near the floor."

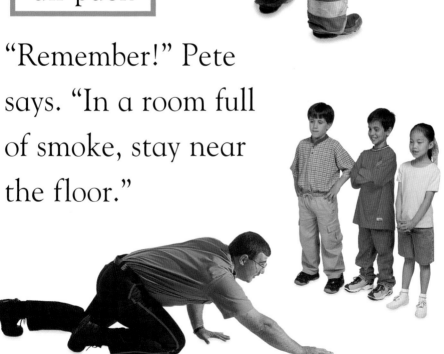

It is almost supper time. Rob
cooks in the fire house kitchen.

Fried fish for twelve
hungry firefighters!

6:00 p.m.

Ring! Ring! Ring!

The fire alarm goes off.
Everyone scrambles!

Rob is ready
to go.

The fire engine
roars out of the station.
EEE–I I I, EEE–I I I
goes the siren.

6:10 p.m.

Pete puts on his mask
and takes the attack
line to the door.
He waits.

mask

Rob is on rescue.

Michelle's dog Pickles is still in the house!

Rob goes in first.
He hears a bark.

He finds
Pickles in
the den.

Rob takes Pickles
to Michelle.

Pete has a radio inside
his helmet. Attack line
one—Go!

helmet

Pete goes in. Soon
water will rush out of
the hose.

The fire is out!

Rob folds
the hose.

hose

Luis helps with
the cleanup.

8:00 p.m.

The chief reports—
the house is safe now.

27

Back at
the station,
everything
is cleaned.

The hose,
the truck...
the firefighters!

10:45 p.m.

Rob cooks again!
At last the firefighters get to eat
their fish dinner. Then it is time
for bed.

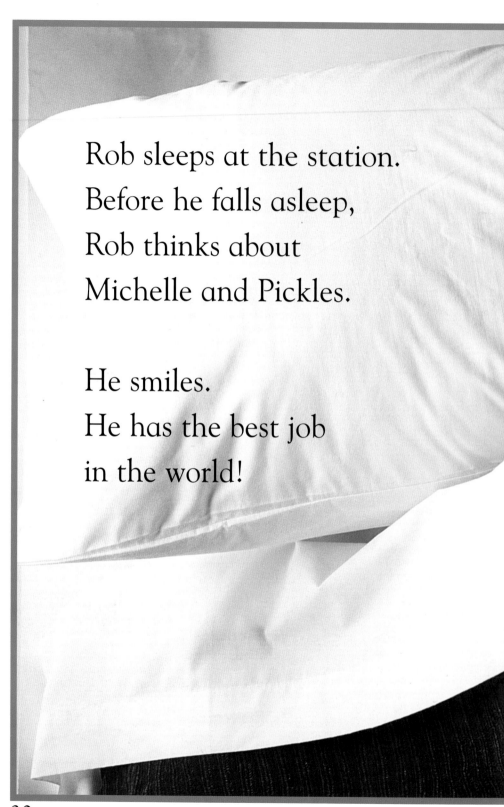

Rob sleeps at the station.
Before he falls asleep,
Rob thinks about
Michelle and Pickles.

He smiles.
He has the best job
in the world!

Picture word list

nozzle
page 6

air pack
page 15

fire exit
page 10

mask
page 20

sprinkler
page 11

helmet
page 24

siren
page 14

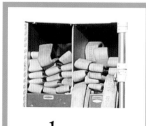

hose
page 26